# THE FIRST MINUTE

## HOW TO START CONVERSATIONS THAT GET RESULTS

# WORKBOOK

CHRIS FENNING

Copyright © 2021 by Chris Fenning

All rights reserved. No part of this book may be reproduced or used in any manner without written permission of the copyright owner except for the use of quotations in a book review.
For more information, address: chris@chrisfenning.com

Select material originally appeared in The First Minute, by Chris Fenning, published by Alignment Group Ltd, London, 2020

The First Minute
How to Start Conversations That Get Results
WORKBOOK
By Chris Fenning

Book cover by Marko Polic & Chris Fenning

Published by: Alignment Group
20-22 Wenlock Road
London
N1 7GU

First paperback edition May 2021

ISBN 978-1-8382440-4-0 (paperback)
ISBN 978-1-8382440-5-7 (ebook)

www.chrisfenning.com

# CONTENTS

INTRODUCTION — 1
HOW TO USE THIS WORKBOOK — 1

## SECTION ONE

THE FIRST MINUTE FUNDAMENTALS — 3
FRAMING SINGLE TOPICS — 7
FRAMING MULTIPLE TOPICS — 23
STRUCTURED SUMMARY — 35
TIME CHECK — 53

## SECTION TWO

OTHER USES FOR THE FIRST MINUTE METHODS — 59
EMAILS — 61
MEETINGS AND INVITATIONS — 67
STATUS UPDATES — 77
ESCALATING ISSUES — 87

## APPENDIX

EXTRA PRACTICE TEMPLATES — 93

# INTRODUCTION

This workbook is a companion for "The First Minute: How to start conversations that get results".

You don't need to have read the whole of *The First Minute* before starting this workbook, but you will get more value from these activities if you are already familiar with the methods described in the main book.

Each chapter of this workbook contains some content from *The First Minute*. This is to introduce and explain the various activities and should save you having to switch back and forth between the two books for each activity.

Communication is not a natural ability; it is a learned skill. The best way to learn a skill is to practice in a deliberate and repeatable way that forms good habits. This workbook will help you do that.

*The First Minute* is available to buy online and from your favorite bookstores. You can also pick up a copy at www.chrisfenning.com/books.

# HOW TO USE THIS WORKBOOK

In this workbook you will apply the methods described in *The First Minute* to a range of work situations. This includes: Conversations, emails, meeting invites, meeting introductions, status updates, and escalations. These are the types of situation that make up 80% of our work communication.

To get the most out of this workbook I suggest completing the activities in section 1 in the order they appear. This will help you learn the fundamental methods to get the first minute right. In section 2 you will practice applying the fundamentals to a range of work situations. You can choose to complete the activities in section 2 in any order, based on your specific goals and needs.

You can either read the whole of *The First Minute* before starting this workbook, or you can work through the chapters in *The First Minute* at the same time as doing the activities in this book. You can also return to this workbook whenever you come across work related communication that you feel could have been better.

That being said, we all learn in different ways so pick whatever approach suits your style of learning.

## A NOTE ABOUT LAYOUT

The content of this workbook is not laid out in the same order as the content in *The First Minute*.

- The main book covers all the theory related to framing in a single chapter. The theory for creating a structured summary is in another chapter. Each chapter contains both fundamental and advanced techniques.
- This workbook splits the methods and exercises for both framing and structured summary into separate chapters for fundamental and advanced techniques.

This approach helps you become comfortable with the core principles of framing and structured summary. Then you can move on to the more complex and nuanced applications of each method.

If that sounds complicated, don't worry. Each section of this workbook references the relevant chapters and pages from *The First Minute* to help you keep track of where you are.

> This book is supplemented by pdfs and other downloads. Download your copies today from: www.chrisfenning.com/resources

# SECTION ONE

## THE FIRST MINUTE FUNDAMENTALS

*(Reference The First Minute pages 1 – 80)*

## SECTION ONE INTRODUCTION

Creating the most effective first minute of any work conversation is a two-step process.

- **Step 1:** Frame the conversation in fifteen seconds or less. Framing provides context, makes your intentions known, and gives a clear headline.
- **Step 2:** Create a structured summary of the entire message you need to deliver. State the goal and define the problem that stands between you and achieving that goal. Then focus the conversation on the solution.

By following these steps, you can start any work conversation feeling confident that you are communicating clearly. This is all possible in less than a minute, no matter how complex the topic.

It doesn't matter what your job title is or what level you occupy in the organization; the activities and exercises in this book will help you become a clearer, more concise, and effective communicator.

---

More information about the importance of starting your communication the right way is available in The First Minute – get a copy at any good bookstore or from www.chrisfenning.com

# WHY IS THE FIRST MINUTE IMPORTANT?

When learning a new method or technique it helps to understand the problem being solved. The questions in this activity help clarify the importance of the first minute for you. They also capture the communication issues you will learn to avoid by practicing the techniques in this workbook.

**Why do you think the first minute is important?**

_____

_____

_____

_____

**What are the consequences of starting a conversation badly?**

_____

_____

_____

_____

**What are the consequences of starting an email in an unclear or long-winded way?**

_____

_____

_____

_____

You should now have a list of consequences from unclear communication. Some may be minor, some might be significant, but it is probably safe to assume that you want to avoid causing any of these consequences in your own communication.

The following activities are designed to give you the simplest and most effective tools to avoid these consequences. Let's get started!

*(Blank page for notes)*

# FRAMING SINGLE TOPICS

*(Reference The First Minute pages 5 - 30)*

*Framing happens in the first fifteen seconds of a conversation.*

The problem with starting conversations about work topics is that we are never taught how to do it. Most professionals have fourteen to eighteen years of schooling and yet don't get a single lesson on how to start conversations about work topics. No wonder we have so many ineffective conversations at work.

**What do you struggle with most when starting a work conversation?**

_____
_____
_____
_____

**When someone talks to you at work, what do you want to know right at the start?**

_____
_____
_____
_____

# WHAT IS FRAMING?

Framing, as defined in *The First Minute*, is the simplest way to prepare an audience to receive your message before you go into detail. Framing lets the audience know what is expected of them right from the start. Clear framing also ensures they understand the core of the message within a few sentences.

**Framing = Context + Intent + Key Message**

- **Context**: This is the topic you want to talk about. Of all the topics in the world, this is the one you will talk about now.
- **Intent**: What you want the audience to do with the information you are about to share.
- **Key message:** The most important part of the overall message you are about to deliver (the headline).

Framing should take no more than three sentences and be delivered in less than fifteen seconds.

The point is to let your audience know what you are going to talk about, so they aren't guessing for the first few minutes of the conversation. If the first lines of your message provide context, intent, and a key message, you will have clearer conversations every time.

The information and activities in this section will help you learn the framing method. You will have lots of chances to practice and will start building the habit of thinking about context, intent, and key message whenever you start communicating at work.

# CONTEXT

*(Reference The First Minute pages 10 - 12)*

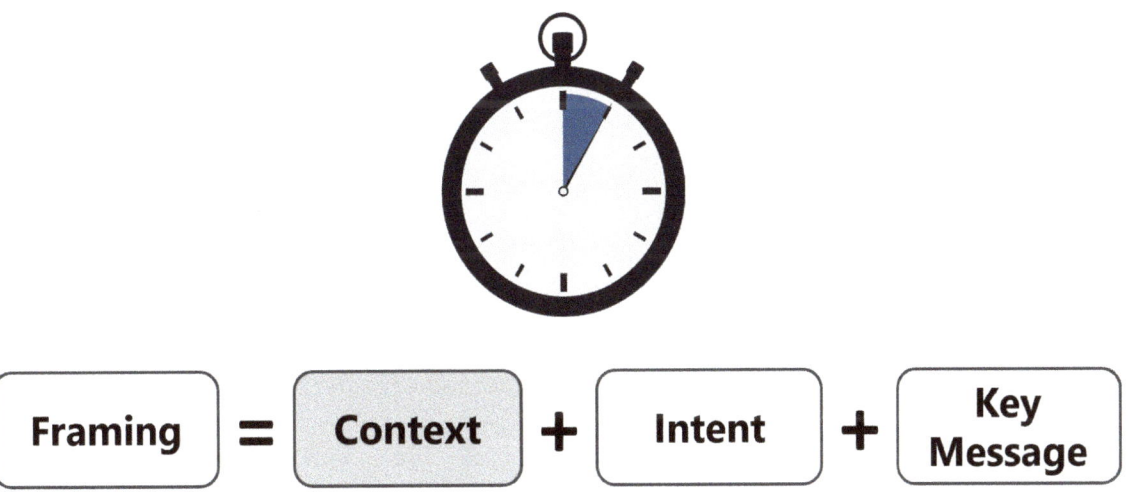

Context is the topic you want to communicate about. Before you start talking about the details of your message, you need to provide some context. You need to orient your audience, so you are both starting at the same point.

This is easy to do if you start your message with a simple statement.

- Name the project or the issue.
- Name the process, system, or tool you will talk about.
- Give the name of the customer with whom you are working.
- Name the task or objective you want to talk about.

The options are endless. The key is to give the context quickly, so your audience knows the topic or area you are going to talk about.

# >> ACTIVITY <<

What are examples of context for your work communication? Write down the context for work conversations you started, or emails you sent, in the last week.

**EXAMPLES OF CONTEXT:**

- I'm working on project ABC . . .
- I read the marketing report you sent me . . .
- The office supplies have arrived . . .
- I want to reward my team . . .
- I'm planning the office party . . .
- The kitchen sink is leaking . . .

*(More examples are available on pages 11 and 12 in The First Minute)*

**CONTEXT 1:** _____

**CONTEXT 2:** _____

**CONTEXT 3:** _____

**CONTEXT 4:** _____

**CONTEXT 5:** _____

**CONTEXT 6:** _____

**CONTEXT 7:** _____

**CONTEXT 8:** _____

**CONTEXT 9:** _____

**CONTEXT 10:** _____

## QUESTIONS TO CONSIDER

- Did you start the conversations/emails with a short statement that made the context clear?
- Are any of these contexts likely to come up again? If yes, make a note of them and you can use the same context statement each time you want to talk about them.

# INTENT

*(Reference The First Minute pages 13 - 19)*

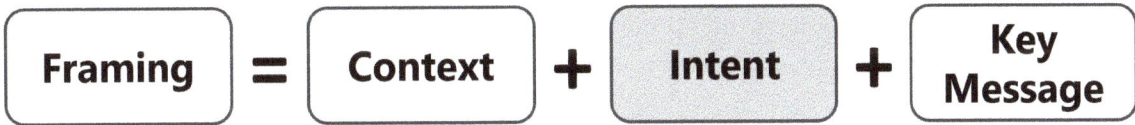

Now that you've provided context and the audience is on the same page as you, it's time to let them know what you need them to do with the information you are about to share.

Most work-related intentions fall into one of the following categories. For each category, it is possible to describe the intent of the message in one line.

- Needing help/advice/input
- Requesting action
- Wanting a decision
- Letting someone know something is about to happen, so they are not surprised
- Providing information/input the other person asked for previously
- Talking for social purposes

*(Activity begins on the next page)*

## >> ACTIVITY <<

In this activity you will reuse the context examples you wrote in the previous activity. For each of the ten context statements, write down the intent. This doesn't need to be written in complete sentences. Just make sure it is clear what you needed, wanted, or expected the other person to do with the information.

**EXAMPLES OF INTENT:**

- Can you help me?
- I need some advice.
- You need to know this before you talk to the client.
- Here's the report you asked for.

*(More examples are available on page 17 in The First Minute)*

| | CONTEXT | INTENT |
|---|---|---|
| 1 | | |
| 2 | | |
| 3 | | |
| 4 | | |

|    | CONTEXT | INTENT |
|----|---------|--------|
| 5  |         |        |
| 6  |         |        |
| 7  |         |        |
| 8  |         |        |
| 9  |         |        |
| 10 |         |        |

### QUESTIONS TO CONSIDER

- Did you make the intent clear when you started the original conversation or email?

If no, this is something to watch out for in the future. You should always know your intent, and make it clear to your audience when you start speaking.

# KEY MESSAGE

*(Reference The First Minute pages 20 - 26)*

After you have provided context and clearly stated your intent, it's time to deliver your key message. Your key message is the one line that contains the most important piece of information your audience needs to know. The key message doesn't have to summarize every detail of the topic you want to talk about, but it should be the most important message you need to communicate.

## >> ACTIVITY <<

Write down the key message for each of the ten topics you used in the "Intent" exercise. These should be written as complete sentences that make sense in relation to the context.

**EXAMPLES OF KEY MESSAGES:**

- "We just closed a new client."
- "Our most experienced developer is leaving."
- "The system is down, and it will take a week to fix."
- "We will finish early."
- "You have been nominated for an award."

*(More key message examples are available on page 25 in The First Minute)*

|   | CONTEXT | KEY MESSAGE |
|---|---------|-------------|
| 1 |         |             |
| 2 |         |             |
| 3 |         |             |
| 4 |         |             |
| 5 |         |             |
| 6 |         |             |

*(Activity continues on the next page)*

| | CONTEXT | KEY MESSAGE |
|---|---|---|
| 7 | | |
| 8 | | |
| 9 | | |
| 10 | | |

### QUESTIONS TO CONSIDER

- Was it easy to identify the key message?
- Do your key messages have a single point?

If you find it difficult to identify the key message, imagine how much harder it is for your audience. They must identify the key message from a longer, less structured introduction without the benefit of the information you have in your head.

If you are trying to communicate multiple points make a note of them. Later in the workbook you will get a chance to practice framing conversations with multiple points. These examples will come in handy.

# PUTTING IT ALL TOGETHER

*(Reference The First Minute pages 27 - 29)*

So far, we've covered the three components of framing: context, intent, and key message. You've seen how each component delivers valuable information, but individually they don't deliver a complete message. This section shows how to put all three components together into short framing statements that will help you start your work conversations quickly and clearly.

This is as simple as it sounds. You will take the three sentences you've created for your message and put them together in two or three lines.

## >> ACTIVITY <<

Pick five of the examples you used in the previous three activities. Then use the five examples to write out the start of each conversation. Write each example in the way you would speak it out loud to someone. Make sure you use complete sentences, not shorthand notes. The value in this activity is to practice framing using your own style of speaking.

For each framing, count the number of words you used and write it in the space provided.

*(A list of framing examples is available on pages 27 - 28 in The First Minute)*

**Conversation 1:** _____

_____

_____

_____

| Number of words used | |
|---|---|


**Conversation 2:** _____

_____

_____

_____

| Number of words used | |
|---|---|

*(Activity continues on the next page)*

**Conversation 3:** _____

_____

_____

_____

| Number of words used | |

**Conversation 4:** _____

_____

_____

_____

| Number of words used | |

**Conversation 5:** _____

_____

_____

_____

| Number of words used | |

**To see how well you are doing, check out the assessment on the next page**

# REVIEW & ASSESSMENT

Let's find out how you did. First, add up the total word count for ALL five of the framing examples you created. Write the number in the box below and check your score against the scale.

| Total number of words used for all 5 framings | |
|---|---|

Less than 100 = Excellent

101 – 149 = Great

150 – 199 = OK

200+ = You would benefit from more practice.

If you scored 150 or more don't worry. You aren't doing badly. Most people take 100 words or more to start a single conversation so anything you got below that is a big step in the right direction.

Total scores of 150+ show you need more practice because your average framing is 30+ words. Any framing with 30 words takes around 20 seconds to say out loud. This length of time is more of a summary than a framing for the conversation. Stick with it. Learning is a journey not a step change, and it takes practice to hone these skills. Take another look at your examples and try to find ways to shorten them to around 20 words each.

**BE CAREFUL**: Low word count by itself doesn't mean the framing is good. These scores are only a guide for how good each framing is. The words you use need to make sense. Make sure you use complete sentences, have decent grammar, etc.

> **TIP**: If you are struggling to keep the word count down, review the examples in *The First Minute* on pages 27-28 and see how you can adjust your own framing to simplify the message.

# HOW WELL DO YOU FRAME REAL CONVERSATIONS?

Now that you've practiced framing conversations, it's time to take a look at how well you do this in your work communication today.

Find the last important email you sent. The longer the email is, the better it will work for this activity. Our memories are not as reliable as we think, and using an email for this activity will help you see exactly what you wrote instead of trying to remember how you started a conversation.

Look at the subject line and the first paragraph of the email.

- Did you provide context?            YES / NO
- Was your intent clear?               YES / NO
- Did you deliver a key message up front?    YES / NO

If you circled YES for each question, well done, you have already been using the core components of good framing (whether you knew it or not!)

If you circled NO for any (or all) of the questions, don't worry. You may not have framed the email perfectly on this occasion, but you now know how to improve the clarity of your next email.

Whether you circled YES or NO to the previous questions, you can still use that example email to practice good framing.

**QUESTION: What would you change to improve the clarity at the beginning of the email?**

Write a new, or revised, beginning to the email. Make sure you include a clear context, intent, and key message.

_____

_____

_____

_____

_____

_____

| Number of words used | |
|---|---|

Is the number of words less than 30? If yes, you are doing great!

> **TIP**: Try putting the context and intent into the subject line of the email. This helps make the topic clear before the email is even opened.

# PREPARING FOR FUTURE COMMUNICATION

It is time to put your new skills to use and apply them to your future work. This activity will help you prepare for conversations that you will have, or emails you will send, in the next week. It will also provide more chances to practice framing conversations for topics directly related to your work.

## >> ACTIVITY <<

Identify the next few topics you need to communicate to your team, boss, or colleagues. For each topic write down a short introduction to the conversation using framing.

This is an opportunity to plan those conversations and be better prepared than if you just started talking or writing. Plus, once you have the framing written down, you can take it with you and use it to start the conversation. No one will fault you for coming prepared to a conversation.

**FRAMING #1**

**Context**: _____

**Intent**: _____

**Key message**: _____

_____

| Number of words used | |
|---|---|

**FRAMING #2**

**Context**: _____

**Intent**: _____

**Key message**: _____

_____

| Number of words used | |
|---|---|

**FRAMING #3**

**Context**: _____

**Intent**: _____

**Key message**: _____

_____

| Number of words used | |
|---|---|

**FRAMING #4**

**Context**: _____

**Intent**: _____

**Key message**: _____

_____

| Number of words used | |
|---|---|

**FRAMING #5**

**Context**: _____

**Intent**: _____

**Key message**: _____

_____

| Number of words used | |
|---|---|

### QUESTIONS TO CONSIDER

- Did you keep the sentences short?
- Are you writing in the same way you speak? While the point of this method is to be brief, it isn't to make you sound artificial.
- Will these framing introductions help make your next conversations clearer?

# FRAMING MULTIPLE TOPICS

*(Reference The First Minute pages 30 - 39)*

Many of our work conversations include more than one topic. While it only takes a little thought and organization to start a conversation clearly with a single topic, it is harder to be clear when talking about multiple topics.

By framing the conversation correctly, it's easier to include multiple topics without the risk of confusion.

# HOW TO TELL IF YOU HAVE MORE THAN ONE TOPIC

*The First Minute* describes how the three parts of framing help clarify the start of your message. It also shows how framing can help you see if you have more than one topic for your conversation.

Start with context. If you can define a separate context for each topic you want to discuss, you have two separate topics to frame. If you want to talk about two different projects, clients, or situations, then you have two topics.

**More than one context = More than one topic of conversation**

**= <u>More than one framing</u>**


If you have reviewed the context and have only one topic, look at your intent. If you need two different actions from your audience, you have two topics. You cannot have a topic that is for information only and also requires an action or decision. These are two different intents, and you should prepare two different messages.

**More than one intent = More than one purpose for the conversation**

**= <u>More than one framing</u>**


If you have a single context and a single intent, the next step is to look at the key message. More often than not, two key messages will need two different framings. It is rare for two different key messages to have the same intent.

**More than one key message**

**= <u>More than one framing</u>**

# HOW TO KEEP TWO TOPICS SEPARATE

Conversations with multiple topics can be framed with a summary framing. The summary framing technique uses the same principles as framing a single topic described in the previous section.

First, create the basic framing for each topic you want to talk about. Remember, separate topics require separate framings. Then, once you have the separate framing for each topic, create an additional summary framing that includes both topics.

This approach frames the overall conversation, preparing the audience for different topics. Each topic is then addressed one at a time as a separate part of the conversation.

At the start of the discussion, the audience knows they will hear about multiple topics. During the conversation the topics are kept separate, each introduced clearly with framing. This makes it much easier for the audience to mentally shift contexts between topics during the conversation.

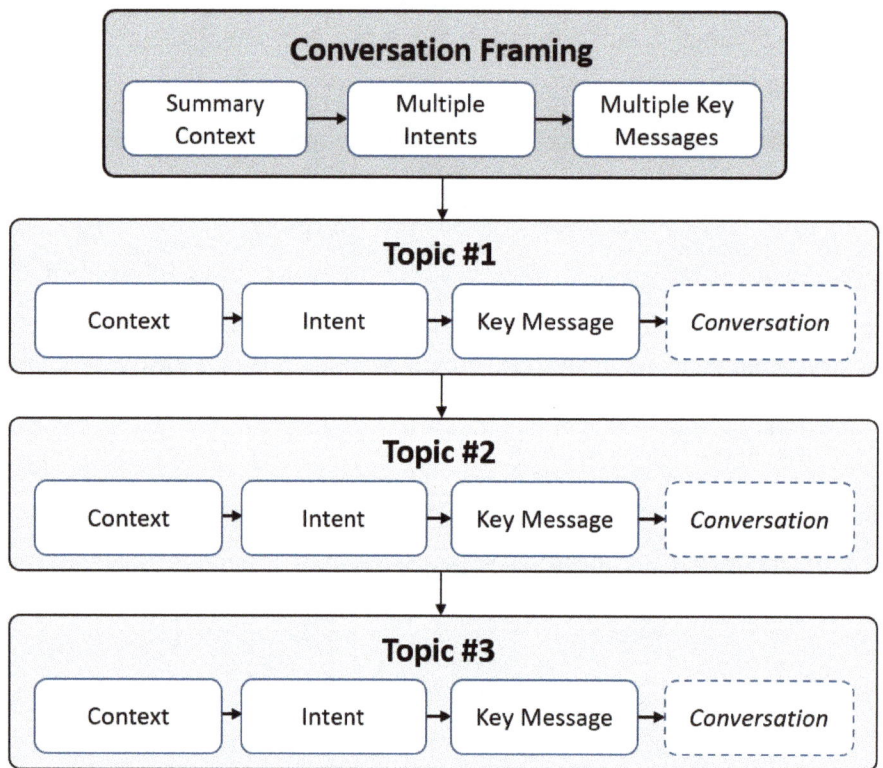

**How to Frame multiple separate topics in one conversation**

## >> ACTIVITY <<

Look at the framing examples you created in the previous activities. Pick two that have different contexts. Write them out below – this shouldn't take long because each framing is ideally less than 20 words.

Then write a summary framing for a conversation that includes both topics. You don't need to aim for the "less than 20 word" target for the summary framing. You should expect to use more words when framing multiple topics together.

Here is an example with three topics to demonstrate the idea. Your activity will use only two topics:

**Example:**

Timothy has three topics to talk to his team leader about.

- Advice about how to handle a problem with a recent delivery
- A decision about nominating a colleague for an award
- A decision about taking time off work

Timothy knew his team leader was busy, so he wanted to be as clear and concise as possible. Here's how he combined the three topics into a single framing:

- **Context**: I'd like to talk to you about three things.
- **Intent**: I need some advice, and I have a couple of decisions.
- **Key message**: We have an issue with the office supplies delivery. I'd like to nominate Dave for an award, and I have a request for some time off.

**FRAMING #1:** *(taken from previous activities)*

**Context**: _____

**Intent**: _____

**Key Message**: _____

_____

*(Activity continues on the next page)*

**FRAMING #2:** *(taken from previous activities)*

**Context**: _____

**Intent**: _____

**Key Message**: _____

_____

Now write a summary framing that introduces the two topics as part of one conversation. Additional space is available for this activity to account for the extra information the summary framing will contain.

**SUMMARY FRAMING:**

**Context**: _____

_____

**Intent**: _____

_____

_____

**Key Message**: _____

_____

_____

_____

## QUESTIONS TO CONSIDER

- Does starting the conversation with a summary framing help keep the topics separate in your mind?
- Will this method be something you use regularly, or occasionally?

# FRAMING MULTIPLE TOPICS WITH THE SAME CONTEXT

We often have more than one point to make or more than one request related to a single topic. This is the situation most likely to cause confusion because it's easy to mix the topics into each other. Framing a conversation to separate topics within one context helps keep separate topics separate.

**Example**: Andrea is a claims adjuster for an insurance company. Her team recently started work in a new region, and she wants to update her boss on the previous week's events. Two topics are at the top of her list, and she has prepared the framing for each topic.

**Topic #1**

- **Context**: New region roll-out.
- **Intent**: Heads-up/FYI.
- **Key Message**: The full-time team is exceeding all their key performance indicators (KPIs).

**Topic #2**

- **Context**: New region roll-out.
- **Intent**: Need a decision.
- **Key Message**: Should we cancel the contract for additional staff?

Andrea prepares an introduction for the conversation that sets up both topics without mixing them up.

> "I have an update on the new region roll-out and have two topics to discuss. One is an FYI about the team's great performance. The other needs a decision about the extra staffing."

Andrea has created an introduction that uses the three components of framing.

- **Context**: An update about the regional roll-out with two topics
- **Intent and Key Message #1:** An FYI about the team's great performance
- **Intent and Key Message #2:** A request for a decision about the extra staffing

In this case, the context of the conversation is having two topics related to the regional roll-out. The intent is clear that one topic is an FYI, and the other needs a decision. A key message is given with each intent to help separate the two topics before Andrea starts providing details.

When starting a conversation with multiple topics related to the same context, the conversation framing provides the single context for everything. After that, you can complete the conversation framing with the separate intent and key messages for each topic.

When the summary is complete, you can deliver Framing #1 or Framing #2 in either order depending on the topic you or your audience would like to discuss first. After completing the first conversation topic, give the framing for the second topic, and complete that conversation. This keeps the two topics separate and prevents confusion.

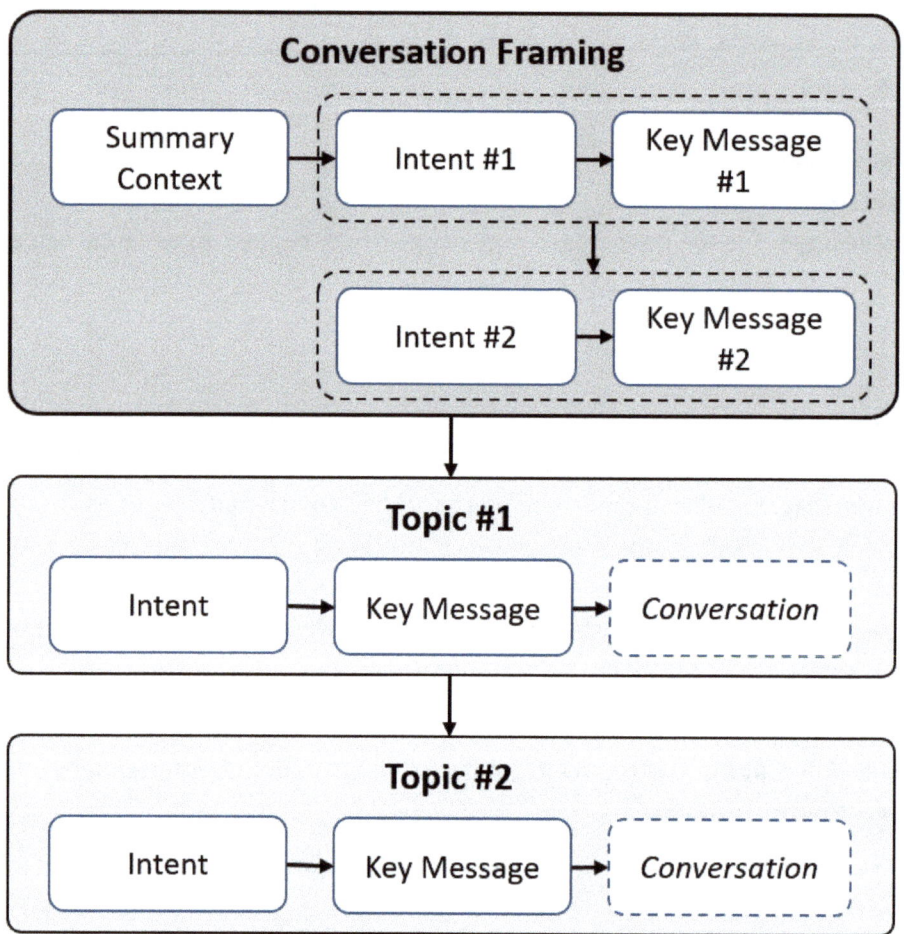

*How to frame multiple topics with the same context in one conversation*

## >> ACTIVITY <<

Review the framing examples you created earlier in this workbook. Pick two that have <u>the same</u> context and write them out below. If you don't have two examples with the same context, pick one from your existing examples then create a new framing with the same context. It can be real or imagined, either is fine for this activity.

Then write a summary framing to introduce a conversation that includes both topics. Again, you don't need to aim for the "less than 20 word" target for the summary framing. You should expect to use more words when framing multiple topics together.

**FRAMING #1:** *(taken from an earlier activity)*

**Context**: _____

**Intent**: _____

**Key Message**: _____

_____

**FRAMING #2:** *(taken from an earlier activity or write a new one)*

**Context**: _____

**Intent**: _____

**Key message**: _____

_____

In the space provided on the next page, write a summary framing that introduces the two topics as part of one conversation. More writing space is available to account for the extra information the summary framing will contain.

*(Activity continues on the next page)*

**SUMMARY FRAMING**

**Single Context:** _____

_____

**Two Intents:** _____

_____

_____

**Two key messages:** _____

_____

_____

_____

_____

## QUESTIONS TO CONSIDER

- Did you feel the need to describe how, or why, the intents or key messages relate to each other?
- Did you state the key messages in the same order as you stated the intents?
- What could you do to make it even more obvious you have different topics to discuss?

Giving descriptions instead of statements is a risk when creating a summary framing. The best way to avoid slipping into description is to focus on making statements of fact. Avoid opinion and background information.

# PREPARING FOR FUTURE CONVERSATIONS WITH MULTIPLE TOPICS

Using examples from past emails and conversations is a great way to practice summary framings. Now that you have more confidence with the method it is time to apply it to communication you will use in the future.

## >> ACTIVITY <<

Think about a work conversation or email you need to have (or send) in the next week, and that includes more than one topic. The topics can have the same context, or different, and the same intent, or different. As long as there are two distinct topics to discuss in the same conversation.

Write down the framing for each topic and then create a summary framing to introduce the two topics in the same conversation.

**FRAMING #1:**

**Context**: _____

**Intent**: _____

**Key message**: _____

_____

**FRAMING #2:**

**Context**: _____

**Intent**: _____

**Key message**: _____

_____

*(Activity continues on the next page)*

Now write a summary framing that introduces the two topics as part of one conversation. More space is available to account for the extra information the summary framing will contain.

**SUMMARY FRAMING**

**Summary Context:** _____
_____

**Summary Intents:** _____
_____
_____
_____

**Key Messages:** _____
_____
_____
_____
_____

Now that you have your summary framing written out, it will be much easier to start the conversation. This simple approach should make the start of the conversation clearer for both you and the audience.

## >> ACTIVITY <<

The section below provides more space to practice creating summary framings. Pick topics that you need to communicate about soon, and that have different context and/or intents. write the summary framing for them.

### SUMMARY FRAMING #1

**Summary context**: _____
_____

**Summary intents**: _____
_____
_____

**Key messages**: _____
_____
_____
_____

### SUMMARY FRAMING #2

**Summary context**: _____
_____

**Summary intents**: _____
_____
_____

**Key messages**: _____
_____
_____
_____

## SUMMARY FRAMING #3

**Summary context:** _____

_____

**Summary intents:** _____

_____

_____

**Key messages:** _____

_____

_____

_____

*(More space for practicing is available at the end of the workbook)*

# STRUCTURED SUMMARY

*(Reference The First Minute pages 41 - 53 and pages 63 - 70)*

*A structured summary comes after framing and fills the remaining forty-five seconds of the first minute.*

Communication courses often tell us to be concise, to start with a summary of the topic, but they rarely show us how to create such a summary. It's one thing to know you should be doing something. It's quite another to know how to do it. The solution to this problem is to create a structured summary using the Goal, Problem, Solution (GPS) method.

The three parts of the structured summary are:

- **Goal**: The goal you are trying to achieve
- **Problem**: The problem that is preventing you from reaching your goal
- **Solution**: What I/we/you are going to do to solve the problem

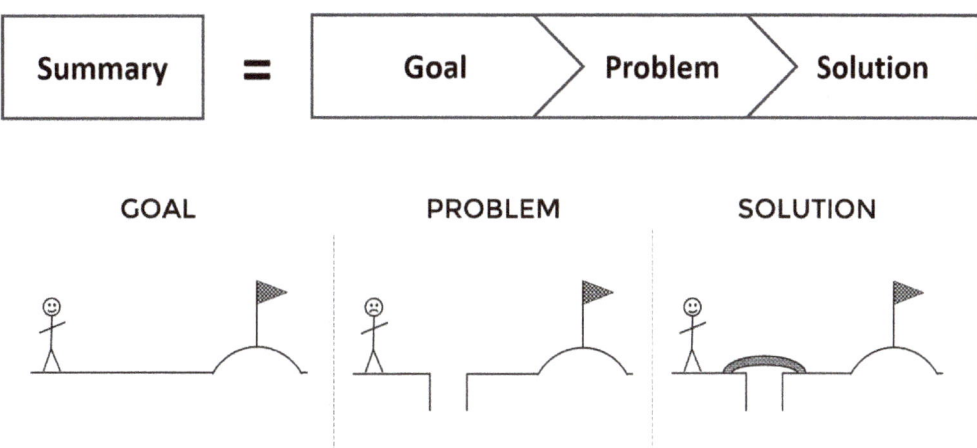

Starting with a good summary is critical to communicating clearly. Without a clear summary, your audience has no frame of reference for the information you are about to share.

# WHAT ARE THE GOALS IN YOUR WORK?

All companies have goals, targets, and deadlines, and most of our daily work effort is about making sure those goals and targets are met. Creating a great summary starts by knowing the goal your topic relates to. Here are some examples of goals people have in their work.

**DAY-TO-DAY GOALS**

- Make sure the office supplies don't run out
- Get time with Jane from accounting to talk about the monthly reports
- Hit the sales targets
- Complete 10 customer tickets every day
- Find a missing order
- Write a report

**LARGE GOALS**

- Ensure the team is meeting their Key Performance Indicators (KPIs).
- Fix the customer support system because it is not working
- Increase customer satisfaction

**ENORMOUS GOALS**

- Win the bid to host the Olympics.
- Build a shopping center/mall
- Acquire another company

Note how short these example goal statements are. It doesn't take many words to state a goal.

There is an important difference between *stating* the goal and *describing* the goal. When we state something it is short, factual, and to the point. When we describe something, we use more words, especially more adjectives.

Describing a goal leads us to include context, background, history, and so on. Those things may or may not be relevant to the discussion. Your audience may already have that information. It is also possible they don't need, or care about it. If the audience wants more information about the goal, they will ask for it. Save yourself time, don't guess what they might want to know, keep it short and to the point.

# >> ACTIVITY <<

Write down some of the goals in your job. This includes regular or recurring goals that make up the core of what you are trying to achieve at work.

Don't fall into the description trap – always state the goal with as few words as necessary. It doesn't take many words to make it clear what the target is.

### DAY-TO-DAY GOALS

*These goals can be completed within a day, or take a week at most.*
*E.g., complete a task, create a document/widget, ensure compliance with X procedure, etc.*

1. _____
2. _____
3. _____
4. _____
5. _____
6. _____
7. _____
8. _____
9. _____
10. _____

### LARGE GOALS

*These goals take weeks or months to achieve.*
*E.g., complete a project, achieve sales target, build a software application, etc.*

What are some examples of large goals you have in your work? Write them in the spaces below.

1. _____
2. _____
3. _____
4. _____
5. _____

This exercise gets you thinking about the goals you have in your job every day. By writing them down you are practicing visualising a goal and writing it simply. We don't often do this. So, getting used to thinking about, and writing down, your regular goals is good practice.

If you are struggling to think of work goals – think about the objectives, tasks, and activities you do every week. Each of these has a defined goal to achieve.

### QUESTIONS TO CONSIDER

- Did you state the goal or describe the goal?
- Did you feel like writing "because…" for any of the goals?
- Do you have goals that frequently repeat?

It is tempting to include background information and history in the goal. But that isn't relevant when stating *what* the goal is. If you wrote "because" in any of your goals, go back and remove it and the explanation you gave. Does removing it make the goal statement clearer?

If you have goals that frequently occur, many of your summaries might start with the same words. Make a note of these repeating goals and you can use these phrases when starting your summaries.

### A NOTE ABOUT TIMEFRAMES IN GOALS

You might want to include a timeframe in the goal statement. For example, "Send the monthly report to Sasha in accounting by Friday." Timeframes can be included in goals, but only where it is relevant to the problem you are trying to solve. If the timeframe isn't relevant to the problem or solution, then it doesn't need to be stated in the goal.

# WHAT PROBLEMS STAND BETWEEN YOU AND YOUR WORK GOALS?

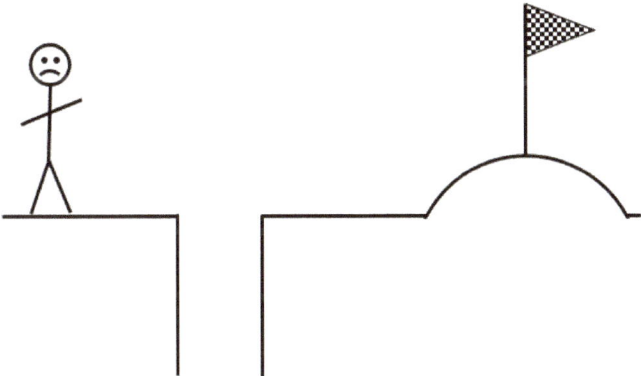

While the purpose of our work is to achieve goals, our day-to-day work is about overcoming the problems that stand between us and the goals.

Problems can be small, like having to manually copy information between documents instead of it being automated. Problems can also be large, like responding to the accidental shutdown of an entire power grid in a city. Whatever job you do, your day is filled with problems to solve.

Each goal can have many problems that prevent it being achieved. These problems are the reason some jobs exist. Here are some possible problems associated with the example goals in the previous section.

### DAY-TO-DAY GOAL EXAMPLES

**GOAL**: Make sure the office supplies don't run out
- **Problem #1**: A large meeting used up all the notepads
- **Problem #2:** The budget has all been spent

**GOAL**: Get time with Jane from Accounting to talk about the monthly reports
- **Problem #1**: Jane is on vacation for 2 weeks
- **Problem #2**: My schedule is full with other work

**GOAL**: Hit the sales targets
- **Problem #1**: The client list is out of date
- **Problem #2**: Our top sales agent left

**GOAL**: Complete 10 customer tickets each day
- **Problem #1**: The first ticket took all day to complete
- **Problem #2**: Staff training took out three hours today

**GOAL**: Find a missing order
- **Problem #1**: There is no order number
- **Problem #2**: The order tracking system is not working

**GOAL**: Write a report
- **Problem #1**: I don't have the right data
- **Problem #2**: I keep being interrupted

## LARGE GOAL EXAMPLES

**GOAL**: Ensure the team is meeting their Key Performance Indicators (KPIs)
- **Problem #1**: The goal is 80% more than last year but the team is the same size
- **Problem #2**: We have four new team members and they are still learning

**GOAL**: Fix the customer support system because it is not working
- **Problem #1**: No one knows why it is broken
- **Problem #2**: It is Saturday and the IT team is not working today

**GOAL**: Increase customer satisfaction
- **Problem #1**: We have no budget to research the causes of customer dissatisfaction
- **Problem #2**: We just had a major service outage and the customers couldn't use our product for three days

## ENORMOUS GOAL EXAMPLES

**GOAL**: Win the bid to host the Olympics.
- **Problem #1**: Other countries are bidding to win it too
- **Problem #2**: We have no existing infrastructure and need to build an entire sports complex

**GOAL**: Build a shopping center/mall
- **Problem #1**: The city council is blocking the planning permission
- **Problem #2**: Some of the land we need is not available to buy

**GOAL**: Acquire another company
- **Problem #1**: The other company doesn't want to be bought by us
- **Problem #2**: We don't have enough cash to buy it

## >> ACTIVITY: DAY-TO-DAY PROBLEMS <<

It doesn't matter how complex or mundane a topic is; it is always necessary to explain the topic in a way that people can quickly absorb and understand.

Write an example of a problem you come across for each of the day-to-day goals you listed earlier.

|   | DAY-TO-DAY GOAL | PROBLEM |
|---|---|---|
| 1 | | |
| 2 | | |
| 3 | | |
| 4 | | |
| 5 | | |

*(Activity continues on the next page)*

## >> ACTIVITY: LARGE PROBLEMS <<

Write an example of a problem you must overcomes for each of the large goals you listed earlier.

| | LARGE GOAL | PROBLEM |
|---|---|---|
| 1 | | |
| 2 | | |
| 3 | | |
| 4 | | |
| 5 | | |

This activity helps you think about the work you do as overcoming problems. Your list should include things that you spend time fixing/solving/addressing as part of your job.

### QUESTIONS TO CONSIDER

- Do your problem statements make sense to other people in your team?
- Would someone outside your team understand the problems you have written?
- Would an executive understand what is making the goal difficult to achieve?

If you answered NO to any of these questions, try rewriting the goal and problem using language that would be understood by people outside your team. Consider the problem from the perspective of the end result, the end user experience, or the outcome.

# WHAT SOLUTIONS DO YOU USE AT WORK?

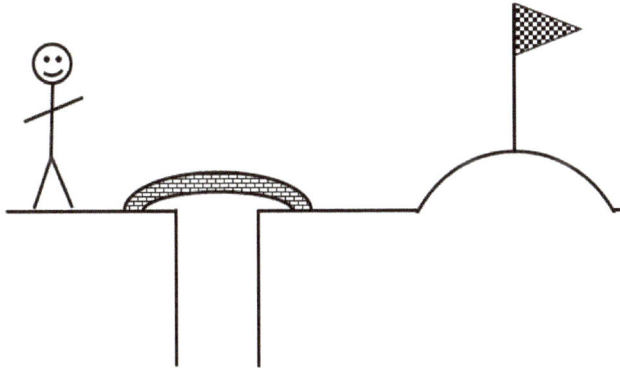

The third part of a structured summary is the solution. The solution statement tells your audience what you want to happen next. Even if you clearly define the goal and the problem, you still need a clear solution statement because, without a solution, your audience is left thinking, "So what?"

If you have used framing, your audience will already know the intent of your message, e.g., making a decision, providing advice or input. The solution statement in the structured summary is where you state what you want to happen next. This tells the audience how they are involved.

Why is this important? The solution statement focuses the audience on the solution, on the path forward. It stops the discussion from getting bogged down in the problem.

Solution discussions fit into one of three categories:

1. You have a problem and need to find a solution.
2. You have a problem and are recommending or reviewing a solution.
3. You had a problem and it is being, or it has been solved, and you are reporting the status.

These three categories are your guide to creating a good solution statement.

If you are in scenario 1 and don't have a solution to your problem, the purpose of the conversation is almost certainly to help you find a solution. In this case, the solution part of your summary should make it clear that you are asking for help and/or input.

If you already have a solution, you are either in scenario 2 or 3.

If scenario 2, your summary is that you have a recommended solution that needs review, approval, or implementation.

If scenario 3, you don't need to describe the solution in the structured summary. Your solution summary is that work is underway to fix the problem, or that the work is done and the problem is solved.

## >> ACTIVITY <<

Now you have clear goals, and you know the problems you solve as a part of your job, it is time to think about the solutions.

For each of the problems listed in the previous activity, what are the solutions? Can you write the solution in one or two sentences?

If you aren't sure what the solution to a given problem is, don't worry, this isn't a test. The solutions you write do not have to be the best solution for each problem. The idea is to practice writing solutions in a single short sentence. You can use this activity to write down any possible solution that makes sense for each problem.

**SOLUTIONS FOR DAY-TO-DAY PROBLEMS**

|   | DAY-TO-DAY PROBLEM | SOLUTION |
|---|---|---|
| 1 | | |
| 2 | | |
| 3 | | |
| 4 | | |
| 5 | | |

## SOLUTIONS FOR LARGE PROBLEMS

For each of the large problems listed in the previous activity, what are the solutions? Can you write the solution in one or two sentences?

|   | LARGE PROBLEM | SOLUTION |
|---|---|---|
| 1 | | |
| 2 | | |
| 3 | | |
| 4 | | |
| 5 | | |

## QUESTIONS TO CONSIDER

- Do you have a solution for every problem? If not, that's okay. Look at page 48 in *The First Minute* for how to write/say a solution statement when the solution is unknown.
- What type of solution discussion are you having in each example? Are you asking for, proposing, or reporting on a solution?
- How easy was it to write a solution in a single sentence?
- Would someone outside your team understand the solution statements? What about someone who doesn't have the same skills or knowledge as you?
- Did you felt the urge to describe the solution, explain how it works, or why it was needed?

Solutions are notoriously difficult to state in a single line. We want to describe solutions at length because we are proud of them, or because we are unsure of them and want input. We describe why we chose a solution to help our audience understand the thinking behind our choice. Or we want to convince the audience of the merit of our choice.

If it was difficult to state the solution in a single line, find more examples and practice writing them as a single sentence statement. Thinking about solutions in a single line is a skill you can learn through practice.

When talking to someone outside your team you should always use language that makes sense to them. The words and phrases that are specific to your job might mean nothing to other people.

We often feel the need to add a lot of information about the solution. However, what the audience needs to hear is a statement that makes it clear what the solution is. The point of a summary is to give a very short overview of the topic. All the other information you want to share might be important, but it can wait until the conversation that follows the summary.

## HOW WELL DO YOU SUMMARIZE TOPICS?

The activities in the previous chapters helped you practice the core summary statements of goal, problem, and solution. Now it's time to take a look at how well you summarize your own work.

If you skipped the previous summary activities, I strongly suggest you go back and do them. The activity here will be more valuable if you have practiced the method.

## >> ACTIVITY <<

Find the last email you sent which shared information about a large or complex topic. Status update emails work well for this activity, and the longer the email is, the better it will work. Our memories are not as reliable as we think, and using an email will help you see exactly what you wrote.

Look at the first paragraph or two of the email and answer these questions:

- Did you include a summary of the whole topic?    YES / NO
- Did you state the goal?    YES / NO
- Did you state the problem you needed to overcome?    YES / NO
- Did you include a simple statement about the solution? *    YES / NO

*Remember, the solution can be a request for help to find a solution. It is a good idea to provide or propose a solution, but if you don't have one then the solution line of the summary is usually a request for help or guidance.*

If you circled YES for each question, well done. You have already been using the core components of a good structured summary (whether you knew it or not!)

If you circled NO for any (or all) of the questions, don't worry. You may not have summarized the topic perfectly on this occasion, but you now know how to improve the next email.

Whether you circled YES or NO to the previous questions, you can still use that example email to practice creating a good structured summary.

What would you change to improve the clarity at the beginning of the email?

_____

_____

_____

_____

_____

Write a new, or revised, beginning to the email. Make sure you include clear goal, problem, and solution statements in the summary.

_____

_____

_____

_____

_____

_____

### QUESTIONS TO CONSIDER

- If you use this new summary as the first paragraph, can you make the original email shorter?
- Does the summary make the purpose of the email clearer?
- Did you frame the original email? If yes, does the framing match the revised summary?

A good summary often enables us to remove other information not related to the solution. The result is shorter, clearer emails. In many cases a summary is all that you need to include. Think how much time you can save if you only have to write a short summary instead of a long email.

# PREPARING FOR FUTURE CONVERSATIONS

Using examples from past emails and conversations is great for practicing creating summaries. Now it is time to apply the structured summary method to communication you will use in the future.

Think about a work conversation or email you need to have (or send) in the next week. Ideally, it should be about something complex or challenging. It should also be a new topic for the person receiving the message.

> *Tip: Status updates work well for this activity*

Write down the goal, problem, and solution statements for your topic. Can you clearly define the goal you are trying to achieve? Is the problem statement focused on the one thing that prevents you from achieving the goal? Do you have a clear solution statement that lets your audience know exactly what you want to happen next?

**GOAL**: _____

_____

**PROBLEM**: _____

_____

**SOLUTION**: _____

_____

_____

_____

You now have your structured summary. The start of the conversation should be shorter and clearer.

## >> ACTIVITY <<

The section below provides more space to practice your structured summaries. Pick topics you need to communicate soon and write the summaries for them. If you are struggling for ideas, start with any updates you need to give in the next two weeks. Updates are one of the best occasions to be concise. Most people want the key information and don't care about the backstory.

### SUMMARY #1:

**GOAL**: _____

_____

**PROBLEM**: _____

_____

**SOLUTION**: _____

_____

_____

_____

### SUMMARY #2:

**GOAL**: _____

_____

**PROBLEM**: _____

_____

**SOLUTION**: _____

_____

_____

_____

## SUMMARY #3:

**GOAL:** _____

_____

**PROBLEM:** _____

_____

**SOLUTION:** _____

_____

_____

_____

## SUMMARY #4:

**GOAL:** _____

_____

**PROBLEM:** _____

_____

**SOLUTION:** _____

_____

_____

_____

*(Activity continues on the next page)*

## SUMMARY #5:

**GOAL**: _____

_____

**PROBLEM**: _____

_____

**SOLUTION**: _____

_____

_____

_____

## QUESTIONS TO CONSIDER

- Did any of your summaries have more than one problem or solution?

We struggle to summarize complex topics when they have many variables and dependencies. Not only that, but we are compelled to mention all of the impacts on other projects, plus any links to other problems.

It is important to remember people can only solve one problem at a time. So, we should only talk about one problem at a time. The goal, problem, solution method helps us focus on a single problem in each summary.

# TIME CHECK

*(Reference The First Minute pages 71 - 80)*

Conversations involve at least two people, the speaker and their audience. Even if you have prepared a fantastic first minute, does your audience have time to talk about it now?

The simplest way to know the answer is to ask, and you should ask in the first minute. There is a key step to take in the first minute to ensure you start the conversation well. The step is called a time check. The time check makes it clear how much time you want from your audience. If you miss this step, you risk damaging your reputation with the person to whom you are talking. If you include it, you will be well on your way to getting the first minute right.

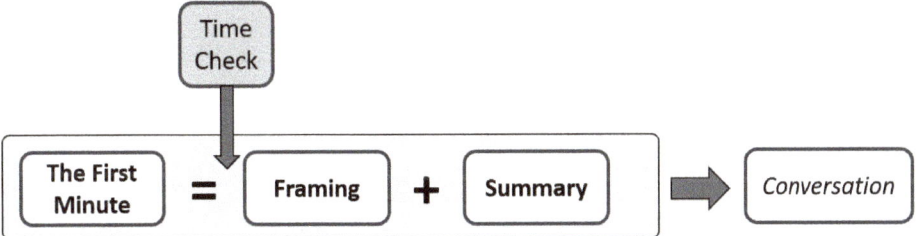

## >> ACTIVITY <<

Think of a work topic you want to talk to someone about. Choose a topic that needs more than a yes or no answer from the audience. It should be a topic requiring a short conversation.

How much time do you think you need for the whole conversation? _____

Now write out the framing for the conversation:

**Context**: _____

**Intent**: _____

**Key Message**: _____

_____

Having written the framing, has your estimate of the time you need changed?   YES/NO

If yes, what is the new estimate of the time you need? _____

Now write the structured summary for the topic.

**GOAL**: _____

_____

**PROBLEM**: _____

_____

**SOLUTION**: _____

_____

_____

_____

### QUESTIONS TO CONSIDER

- Having written the summary, think about the time you need for the whole conversation. Has your estimate of the time you need changed? <u>YES/NO</u>

- Do you think the other person will have questions about the topic? <u>YES/NO</u>

- Did your original estimate include the time it takes to say the framing and the summary? <u>YES/NO</u>

- Consider your answers to the previous three questions. What is the final estimate of the time you need for the conversation? _____

If you completed this activity and your time estimate did not increase, well done. You are probably estimating the time you need well.

On the other hand, if your estimate went up, that's okay. This activity is designed to do two things. Firstly, it shows you that your estimates might need some revision. Secondly, it gives you a simple method to help improve your estimates.

You don't need to work through all these steps before every conversation at work. That would be tedious. But, if you are already thinking of the framing and summary as you prepare to talk to someone, you can use that preparation to check the time you might need.

It takes practice to get into the habit of estimating the right amount of time needed for a conversation. The activity on the next page will help you practice. It uses the framing and summary examples you created earlier in the workbook.

## >> ACTIVITY <<

Look at the framing and summary practices you wrote out in the "Preparing for future conversations" activities in the previous sections.

For each framing, and for each summary, estimate how much time you need for the full conversation. Write your estimates in the table below. When you have the estimates you now know the *minimum* amount of time you should ask for.

| Framing # | Conversation duration estimate |
|---|---|
| 1 | |
| 2 | |
| 3 | |
| 4 | |
| 5 | |

| Summary # | Conversation duration estimate |
|---|---|
| 1 | |
| 2 | |
| 3 | |
| 4 | |
| 5 | |

The estimates in the tables above provide two things:

1. The amount of time you should ask for when starting each one of these future conversations.
2. A set of framing examples from topics common to your job.

These estimates show you the typical time you should ask for when communicating. If you only need a minute for them, then you get to keep asking "Do you have a minute?". If your estimates are longer, you now have a better idea of the typical time you should be asking for.

*(Activity continues on the next page)*

## QUESTIONS TO CONSIDER

- Is the amount of time you estimated in the table more or less than you would have asked for before thinking this way?
- Do you tend to overestimate or underestimate the time you need for conversations?
- Did it help to have the framing when you estimated the time?
- How does thinking about framing & structured summary change your estimates for time? Do they make the estimates longer or shorter?
- Do you feel better prepared after thinking about the likely duration?

I am a chronic under estimator of the amount of time my conversations will take. To counter my own under-estimation, I like to add 20 - 50% more time to my estimate. And if I think I only need a couple of minutes I usually ask for 5 minutes just to be safe.

Consider adjusting your estimates to account for your own natural tendency. And remember, asking for more time than you need and finishing early is much better than the opposite.

# END OF SECTION ONE

## Well done!

You have completed the activities for The First Minute fundamentals.

In this section of the workbook, you practiced the three methods that make up The First Minute:

- Framing
- Structured Summary
- Time Check

You have seen how these methods make your communication clearer and more concise. In addition, the activities about future conversations and emails have given you templates. These are scripts you can use in your work conversations in the coming days and weeks.

The learning and practice don't stop here. If you keep applying the techniques to real conversations and emails it gets easier. Soon you will apply the structures to your introductions without thinking about them.

*\*\*\**

In Section 2 you will practice applying these same methods in a variety of work situations. You'll practice the methods in meeting invites, and meeting introductions. You will also see how presentations, status updates, and escalations are all easier.

While Section 1 was best done by following the activities in sequence, you can complete Section 2 in any order you like. The topics are self-contained. I suggest you try all of them, but you can choose to focus on the areas that are most relevant or interesting to you.

**Are you enjoying this book?**

The best way to thank an author is to post a review on Amazon!

(Please and thank you!)

# SECTION TWO

## OTHER USES FOR THE FIRST MINUTE METHODS

## WAIT !!

If you haven't completed Section 1 yet, go back and finish the activities there before continuing.

Section 2 is best done when you have a good understanding of the fundamental methods.

*(Reference The First Minute pages 81 – 107)*

# INTRODUCTION

As noted at the end of Section 1, the techniques in this book are relevant to more than just verbal communication. Emails, meeting invitations, escalations, and more are all improved using these simple techniques.

This section shows how to apply framing and structured summary in the following situations:

- Writing emails
- Creating meeting invitations
- Giving status updates
- Escalating issues

Unlike Section 1, this section can be completed end-to-end or in whatever order you like. Pick the topics that are most relevant or interesting. Each of the topics is self-contained and not dependent on the other activities in the section.

---

### BONUS DOWNLOAD

The First Minute methods are also powerful tools when it comes to interviews. Head over to www.chrisfenning.com/tfminterviews and download a practical guide for applying these methods to give great interview answers.

# EMAILS

*(Reference The First Minute pages: 81 - 89)*

Email has replaced conversation as the primary means of communication at work. But, it hasn't changed the need to be clear and concise. Luckily, the framing and structured summary methods apply to emails just as they do to conversations. This can reduce the length of an email and greatly increase the clarity of the message.

The email example below shows how framing and strcutured summary can add clarity.

---

**To**: Diane@work.com

**Subject**: Website updates – priority decision needed

Hi Diane,

Can you help me with a priority order decision for the website development team?

**Goal**: The product team has asked us to fix a problem with the login screen on the website.

**Problem**: We have limited resources on our team, and another piece of work would have to move to a later delivery date for this change to occur.

**Solution**: Can you help me understand the priority for the following items? Which one can be delayed?

- Item #1: Layout changes for sidebar menus on the homepage
- Item #2: Automate the generation of the PDFs
- Item #3: Add a question form to the contact page

We have until Friday to decide on what to delay, so you have a couple of days. Please call me if you have any questions.

Thanks,

Chris

# HOW TO STRUCTURE CLEARER EMAILS

Long, unbroken text is difficult to read. The simplest way to break up a block of text and make it easier to read is to add headings, bullets, and white space. This is where the framing and structured summary techniques provide yet another benefit; they provide the headings and bullet-point structure to create a clear message that is visually easy to consume.

A general format for applying framing and structured summaries to an email is the following:

- Context goes in the subject line.
- Intent can go in the subject line or in the first line of the email.
- Your key message should be stated in the first line of the email.
- The goal, problem, and solution are labeled bullet points. You don't need to write the labels, but it does help make the message clearer.

## >> ACTIVITY <<

Find a long email you have sent someone. It should include large blocks of text and little formatting. Use the principles of framing and structured summary to reorganize the email. This will improve the visual clarity of the message.

There is no space for this activity allocated in this workbook. I don't believe that writing out emails by hand is fun. So, for this exercise, you should work in whatever email client you generally use. Create a draft email, copy the example you want to use, and make the structure and layout changes there.

An example email is included on the previous page to show how the formatting can be improved.

### QUESTIONS TO CONSIDER

- Did changing the structure of the email lead to any changes in the content?
- Did using a structure change the purpose of the message?
- Did using a structure make the email shorter? (Did you remove content that didn't fit with the structure?)

## NOT EVERY EMAIL NEEDS A SUMMARY

Every email should be framed. The subject line, and the first line of the email, must provide context, intent, and the key message. But not every email needs to include a summary using the goal, problem, solution (GPS) method.

The best times to use a summary in an email are:

- At the start of a new topic/conversation. (Providing you need to convey more than a one-line update or question)
- When forwarding email chains to someone new.
- When asking for clarification in the middle of a long chain that has lost its way.

## >> ACTIVITY <<

Not every email needs a structured summary. Can you write down some examples of when not to use a structured summary? *(Tip: see page 84 in The First Minute for examples)*

- _____
- _____
- _____
- _____
- _____

# EMAIL CHAINS

There is one situation when it is always a good idea to include a structured summary in an email chain, and that is when forwarding email chains. If you are sending an email chain to someone new, don't make the recipient dig for information. And never make them guess why you are sending it to them. You shouldn't expect them to read the whole thing from the beginning either.

When you forward an email chain, write your email as though you are starting a new conversation. This is because you are. Provide context, have a clear intent for sending the email, and clearly state the key message the recipient needs to know. Then summarize the information.

Without a summary, there is a high chance the recipient either won't read the chain. Or, they will not get the specific point you want them to understand. No matter what, a forwarded email chain should always, always include a summary from you.

## >> ACTIVITY <<

Find a long email chain – at least five emails long, ideally more than ten. Use the template below to draft an email to your manager telling them about the email chain. Create a framing for the topic and write the summary using goal, problem, solution. If there isn't a clear intent, make one up, this is just for practice.

| To | |
|---|---|
| **Subject** | |
| **Body of email** | |
| | |

## QUESTIONS TO CONSIDER

- What do you think when you receive an email chain without an introduction or summary?
- Which would you prefer, to receive forwarded emails with one line "you should see this", or with a good framing and a structured summary?
- Do you think writing a framing and structured summary will reduce the number of email chains you forward?

## >> ACTIVITY<<

The following pages have space to practice this technique. Write out more email chain summaries if you have them.

### SUMMARY INTRODUCTION FOR A FORWARDED EMAIL CHAIN #1

| To | |
|---|---|
| Subject | |
| Body of email | |
| | |

## SUMMARY INTRODUCTION FOR A FORWARDED EMAIL CHAIN #2

| To | |
|---|---|
| Subject | |
| **Body of email** | |

## SUMMARY INTRODUCTION FOR A FORWARDED EMAIL CHAIN #3

| To | |
|---|---|
| Subject | |
| **Body of email** | |

# MEETINGS AND INVITATIONS

*(Reference The First Minute pages: 90 - 99)*

Meetings are a standard part of working life for many people. The process of attending a meeting begins with receiving an invitation. But, if the purpose of the meeting isn't clear when someone reads the invitation, they won't know why they are invited. It won't be clear if any preparation is needed. And it won't be easy to prioritize the meeting against anything else booked for the same time slot.

A meeting invitation is the equivalent of the start of a conversation. You wouldn't walk up to a co-worker and tell him or her to be in a specific location at a certain time. Not without providing some context and a reason to be there. If you wouldn't talk like that in person, don't do it in electronic communication either.

Everyone invited to a meeting wants to know the purpose of the meeting and what will come out of it. The output can be a decision, a more-informed group of people, a list of ideas, solutions, and so on. Whatever the output, it should be clear to every attendee what they will produce in the meeting. The expected output should be clear in the invitation.

Framing is a great way to start a conversation in person. By replacing the key message with two new elements, framing is also a great way to create meeting invitations.

## HOW TO ADAPT FRAMING FOR MEETING INVITATIONS

Start with the first two parts of the standard framing method – Context & Intent. Then change the key message into two separate parts - meeting purpose and meeting output.

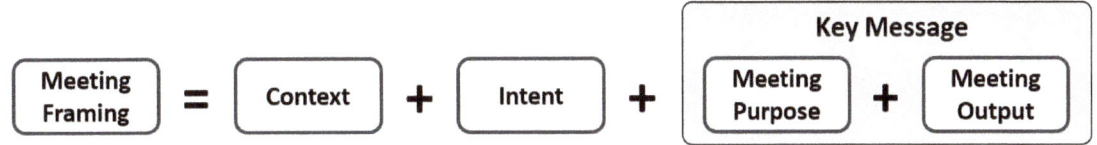

This is where to include each part of framing in the meeting invite:

- **Context:** Include it in the subject line.
- **Intent:** Include it in the subject line.
- **Key Message** is replaced by two new items:
    - **Meeting purpose:** One line describing what the meeting is for.
    - **Meeting output:** One line stating the expected outcome or output of the meeting.

A structured summary can give more information after the meeting output line. This provides a concise summary of the meeting topic to help people prepare.

## EXAMPLE #1

| To | colleagues@work.com |
|---|---|
| Meeting date/time | 01/01/2021 |
| Subject | New project kick-off – need to identify people to work on it |
| **Body of meeting invite** ||

**Meeting Purpose:** To kick off a new software upgrade project and identify resources to work on it.

**Meeting Output:** A short list of the people needed to work on the project.

**Summary info / Background / etc:** *[Structured summary should be included here]*

## EXAMPLE #2

| To | colleagues@work.com |
|---|---|
| Meeting date/time | 01/01/2021 |
| Subject | Health-and-safety rule change – we need to prepare for the changes |
| **Body of meeting invite** ||

**Meeting Purpose:** To review the health-and-safety guideline changes and create a plan to implement them in our department.

**Meeting Output:** A list of actions for us to implement the new health-and-safety guidelines.

**Summary info / Background / etc:** The company HQ has sent out new health-and-safety guidelines. We have one month to prepare before the new rules are enforced. The changes are not significant, but we need to make sure we are ready.

**Additional Information:** *[Structured summary could be included here if needed]*

The person sending the second example chose to keep the key message in the framing as well as the meeting purpose and output. This gives some background information that may help invitees understand the situation better. It is a half way step between having no extra information and including a structured summary. You may choose to do this instead of adding a full structured summary if the key message is sufficient for the invitees to have a clear understanding of the meeting.

As these examples show, it doesn't take much to show recipients why they are invited. In only two or three bullet points, you can provide good introductory content. You can define the purpose of the meeting, and ensure the invitees know why they are invited.

> **TIP**: When using the structure above, keep the bolded words in the invite. They guide readers through the message and make it easier to understand.

# HOW WELL DO YOU WRITE YOUR MEETING INVITATIONS?

Look at your work calendar and find 5 recent meetings that <u>you</u> organized and sent the invitation for. If you don't have any meetings of your own you can use invitations sent by other people. But this activity is better when using your own examples.

Look at each invitation you sent:

- Do the invitations have information in the main body?  YES / NO
- Did you consistently include a clear intent?  YES / NO
- Did you state the meeting purpose?  YES / NO
- Did you state the desired outcome or output?  YES / NO
- Did you include a simple summary of the topic?  YES / NO

If you circled YES for each question, well done. You have already been creating good meeting invitations.

If you circled NO for any (or all) of the questions, don't worry. You will have plenty of chances to practice applying these methods in the next activity.

*\* If you are using invitations written by other people, you can still answer the questions, but do so as an assessor of the other person's content.*

**QUESTION**: What parts of meeting invitation framing do you need to improve?

_____

_____

_____

_____

_____

_____

## >> ACTIVITY <<

Re-write each of the five meeting invitations using the framing method for meetings. Make sure you include a clear purpose and output statements in the body of the invitation. If applicable, you should add a structured summary too. A little extra practice for structured summaries is always good!

### MEETING INVITATION #1

| To | |
|---|---|
| **Meeting date/time** | |
| **Subject** | |
| **Body of meeting invite** | |

**Meeting Purpose:**



**Meeting Output:**



**Summary info / Background / etc.:**



*(Activity continues on the next page)*

## MEETING INVITATION #2

| To | |
|---|---|
| Meeting date/time | |
| Subject | |
| **Body of meeting invite** | |
| Meeting Purpose: <br><br> Meeting Output: <br><br> Summary info / Background / etc.: <br><br><br><br> | |

## MEETING INVITATION #3

| To | |
|---|---|
| Meeting date/time | |
| Subject | |
| **Body of meeting invite** | |
| Meeting Purpose: <br><br> Meeting Output: <br><br> Summary info / Background / etc.: <br><br><br><br> | |

## MEETING INVITATION #4

| To | |
|---|---|
| **Meeting date/time** | |
| **Subject** | |
| **Body of meeting invite** ||
| **Meeting Purpose:** <br><br>**Meeting Output:** <br><br>**Summary info / Background / etc.:** ||

## QUESTIONS TO CONSIDER

- Does using framing make the purpose of the meeting clearer?
- Do you think people will have a better idea of what you expect if the invite uses framing?

# PREPARING FOR FUTURE MEETINGS

Using examples from previous meetings is great for practicing creating invites. Now you have seen framing applied to past invitations it is time to use it for your future invitations.

Pick two meetings you will have in the next few weeks. You can use meetings that you have yet to send invites for. You can also use meetings where you have already sent out the invitations. One of the great things about modern calendar systems is you can easily update an invitation. No one is likely to complain if they receive an updated invite that helps them prepare for the meeting.

For each meeting invite, write it using the modified framing method. Include the context, the intent, the meeting purpose, and the meeting output.

When you have completed this activity, you will have examples of well written invites ready to send. You will also have learned a method you can apply to every meeting invitation you send from now on.

*(You can complete this activity here or in the application you use to send meeting invites)*

## MEETING INVITATION #1

| To | |
|---|---|
| **Meeting date/time** | |
| **Subject** | |
| **Body of meeting invite** | |
| **Meeting Purpose:**<br><br>**Meeting Output:**<br><br>**Summary info / Background / etc.:** | |

## MEETING INVITATION #2

| To | |
|---|---|
| Meeting date/time | |
| Subject | |
| **Body of meeting invite** | |

**Meeting Purpose:**


**Meeting Output:**


**Summary info / Background / etc.:**




## QUESTIONS TO CONSIDER

- Do you feel better prepared for the meeting after writing the framed meeting invite?
- Could you use the meeting invite to kick off the meeting? (to remind the attendees of the purpose)
- Does clarifying the meeting purpose help to identify the best people to invite?

---

### BONUS DOWNLOAD

*Visit www.chrisfenning.com/resources and download*
*an agenda template built to use Framing*

Framing can also help create clear and specific meeting agendas. Instead of listing topics and speakers, frame each topic with at least the context and intent. That way everyone knows what you will cover and why. If you have space, add the key message and really help the attendees prepare.

*(Blank page for notes)*

# STATUS UPDATES

Status updates account for a lot of wasted time in meetings. The worst culprits are project meetings where each team describes the work done since the last meeting.

If you want to stand out, give your updates using the framing and structured summary methods. This also helps make those meetings more productive. As a bonus, this method works for all types of updates outside of meetings.

**STEP 1: Frame each separate update, and ensure the context, intent, and key message are clear.**

No matter how many topics you need to talk about, each status update requires its own framing. When talking about multiple topics, use the method for framing multiple topics. (see Section 1 for activities to improve framing multiple topics together)

Status updates either relate to ongoing work or work done in the recent past. Status updates for future work are the same as giving a status for ongoing work. This is because all updates should focus on the action and the next steps to address an issue or achieve a goal.

**STEP 2: Give a short structured summary – that is the main body of the update.**

Structured summaries for status updates should follow the goal, problem, solution method. You had plenty of practice with that method in Section 1. The goal, problem, solution method ensures your update is given at a good level for any type of audience.

- **Goal**: If the audience isn't familiar with your work the goal statement will help clarify what your update is about.
- **Problem**: If the audience knows the goal but are not familiar with the problem, they will get that info in the short problem statement.
- **Solution**: Focus the majority of the update on the solution and next steps. If the goal and problem are too long you risk wasting time on things the audience already knows.

That being said, the less the audience knows about the goal or the problem, the longer those statements should be. The goal and problem statements must have enough detail to inform the audience. If they don't, the solution won't make sense. After giving a goal and problem statement, the majority of the summary should be on the solution. That's where the value of the discussion is.

**STEP 3: Ask if there are any questions or if more detail is needed.**

After the summary, ask if anyone has questions or wants more detail. This is a "validation checkpoint". It tells you if your goal and problem statements had the right level of detail. By adding this checkpoint, your audience can ask questions if they need more detail.

Instead of assuming the audience needs more information, ask them if they need more. You'll be surprised how often the answer is no! Even if you oversimplify the summary, you will still provide a better introduction to your topic than if you had no summary at all.

# FOCUS ON SOLUTIONS NOT PROBLEMS

Avoid long problem descriptions when giving status updates. Especially when updating people above you in the organization. The audience's first question is likely to be, "what is being done to fix the problem?" As they say in the entertainment industry: Give the audience what they want. Don't spend time dwelling on problems; focus on solutions.

It is also tempting to give long descriptions of the solution. This is understandable; it's a chance to show off the good work you and your team are doing. But, the main thing the audience wants to know is if the problem is fixed yet, and if not, when will it be fixed. They also want to know who is doing what to fix the problem. So tell them, but keep it brief.

If you are describing a solution that is a future plan of action, keep the description short. Make sure you summarize only the key points. Unless asked to do so, do not walk through every step of a plan to fix a problem. Give a summary, and then allow the audience to ask questions about the details. If they want to know more, they will ask.

---

## ONE MINUTE MIGHT BE ENOUGH

Try giving status updates in less than a minute. Use framing and a structured summary to condense the update. You will be surprised how well managers receive these short updates.

Why does this work? We often give status updates with details about every step that caused an issue. Then we talk about the steps we will take to solve the issue. We also describe all the things that we fixed to get to the current status of "good" or "green." For some reason, we believe our managers or our teams care about, or need to know, every last detail. They don't.

In most cases, a one-minute summary of the status is all the audience needs to hear.

# >> ACTIVITY <<

In this activity, you will re-write a status update using goal, problem, and solution. Read the status example below and write a revised version in the space provided.

**Example**: A manufacturing plant had an accident that caused them to shut down production for a day. The foreman was reporting on the situation to the plant manager.

> "We were finishing the BAC-15 production run when the sheet-metal roller jammed. We had to stop the production line while we worked out what happened. Turns out the feeder lines were moved to make room for the installation of a new machine, and they weren't put back properly before production resumed. The teams used the original floor markings to align the rollers, but the lines hadn't been updated to account for the new layout for the new machine to fit. When we found that out, we had to repaint all the floor markings, which isn't a quick job. The safety guideline books are also out of date and need revising to account for the new layout. Anyway, we got it done, and production has resumed."

Write a structured summary for this example in the space below.

**Goal**: _____

_____

**Problem**: _____

_____

**Solution**: _____

_____

_____

_____

*(An example of a rewritten summary is on the next page – try not to look at it until after you've attempted this activity)*

**Example answer:**

> *"We were finishing the BAC-15 production run when the sheet-metal roller jammed. We found and fixed the cause of the jam and had everything up and running again in twenty-four hours. We've already made changes to the production layout and are updating the process documents to make sure this doesn't happen again."*

This is *one* way to rewrite the example using the GPS method. There are many possible versions. Your version may use different words but it should convey the same key points.

- **Goal**: Finish the BAC-15 production run
- **Problem**: The sheet-metal roller jammed
- **Solution**:
  - Found and fixed the cause of the jam
  - Had everything up and running again in twenty-four hours
  - Already made changes to the production layout
  - Updating the process documents to make sure it doesn't happen again

The original status buried the solution in a list of problems and their causes. In the rewritten version, the solution statement is a positive future-looking update. Steps were taken to fix the problem, the production line is running again, and the issue shouldn't happen again.

If you need to give a status update, especially about an issue, focus on the steps already taken to fix the problem. If you haven't taken any steps already, you can summarize the steps you will take to solve the problem. If you don't know what steps to take, the intent of the conversation is probably to get input to help find the solution. This last scenario makes the solution statement simple: "Can you help me fix the problem?"

Keep the solution in a positive direction. It will prevent the conversation from being a negative walk through the history of a problem. And will turn it into a positive, future-looking communication.

## QUESTIONS TO CONSIDER

- Did you include a list of all the problems and/or causes in your summary? Did you need to?
- Does your summary convey a general sense of problems, or that things are back on track?

It is easy to focus on problems when reporting about a negative event. But, if the issues are already fixed, or being fixed, the update should be good news. Sure, you need to consider the impact of the issues, but that doesn't mean you need to focus on what caused the problem. Summarize the issue, describe the solution, and move on.

## >> ACTIVITY <<

Prepare your next status updates in the space below. Use only framing, a structured summary, and a validation checkpoint. Add nothing else. You may be surprised at how few questions you get and how much shorter the status update meeting is.

Before writing the status update, identify the type of solution statement you need:

1. You have a problem and a need to find a solution [FIND]
2. You have a problem and are recommending or reviewing a solution [RECOMMEND / REVIEW]
3. You had a problem, it has been solved, and you are reporting the outcome [REPORT]

When you understand your solution type it is easier to write a clear solution statement.

### STATUS UPDATE #1

**CONTEXT**: _____

**INTENT**: _____

**KEY MESSAGE**: _____
_____

**GOAL**: _____
_____

**PROBLEM**: _____
_____

**SOLUTION**: _____
_____
_____
_____

**VALIDATION CHECKPOINT QUESTION**: _____
_____

### QUESTIONS FOR THIS STATUS UPDATE

- What was the type of solution in your status update?    FIND / RECOMMEND / REPORT
- Does your summary make it clear what the audience's role is in the next steps for the solution?    YES/NO

## STATUS UPDATE #2

**CONTEXT:** _____

**INTENT:** _____

**KEY MESSAGE:** _____

_____

**GOAL:** _____

_____

**PROBLEM:** _____

_____

**SOLUTION:** _____

_____

_____

_____

**VALIDATION CHECKPOINT QUESTION:** _____

_____

## QUESTIONS FOR THIS STATUS UPDATE

- What was the type of solution in your status update?    <u>FIND / RECOMMEND / REPORT</u>
- Does your summary make it clear what the audience's role is in the next steps for the solution?    <u>YES/NO</u>

## STATUS UPDATE #3

**CONTEXT:** _____

**INTENT:** _____

**KEY MESSAGE:** _____

_____

**GOAL:** _____

_____

**PROBLEM:** _____

_____

**SOLUTION:** _____

_____

_____

_____

**VALIDATION CHECKPOINT QUESTION:** _____

_____

## QUESTIONS FOR THIS STATUS UPDATE

- What was the type of solution in your status update?     FIND / RECOMMEND / REPORT
- Does your summary make it clear what the audience's role is in the next steps for the solution?     YES/NO

*(Activity continues on the next page)*

## STATUS UPDATE #4

**CONTEXT:** _____

**INTENT:** _____

**KEY MESSAGE:** _____

_____

**GOAL:** _____

_____

**PROBLEM:** _____

_____

**SOLUTION:** _____

_____

_____

_____

**VALIDATION CHECKPOINT QUESTION:** _____

_____

## QUESTIONS FOR THIS STATUS UPDATE

- What was the type of solution in your status update?   <u>FIND / RECOMMEND / REPORT</u>
- Does your summary make it clear what the audience's role is in the next steps for the solution?   <u>YES/NO</u>

## STATUS UPDATE #5

**CONTEXT**: _____

**INTENT**: _____

**KEY MESSAGE**: _____
_____

**GOAL**: _____
_____

**PROBLEM**: _____
_____

**SOLUTION**: _____
_____
_____
_____

**VALIDATION CHECKPOINT QUESTION**: _____
_____

## QUESTIONS FOR THIS STATUS UPDATE

- What was the type of solution in your status update?     FIND / RECOMMEND / REPORT
- Does your summary make it clear what the audience's role is in the next steps for the solution?     YES/NO

## QUESTIONS TO CONSIDER FOR THIS ACTIVITY

- Does this approach improve your status updates?
- Will your updates be shorter or longer with this approach?

*(Blank page for notes)*

# ESCALATING ISSUES

Escalations happen when you need someone above you to take action. Or you want them to be aware of a situation. Framing and structured summaries are essential for good escalations because:

- You get to the point faster.
- Framing and structured summaries are fact-based. This reduces the chance of using emotion and giving excuses. This makes it easier for the person receiving the escalation to assess the situation.
- Structured summaries focus on solving the problem. This ensures the escalation isn't just a complaint about something that isn't good. It actually lays out a plan that focuses on what to do about the problem.

If the escalation is verbal, create the summary ahead of time, write it down, and take it with you. Don't skip any steps, especially not the solution. That is the key to the whole message in an escalation.

If you are sending an escalation email, follow the approach described in the earlier section "How to use The First Minute methods in emails". This will ensure the email is clear and well organized.

## >> ACTIVITY <<

Practice writing escalations using the templates below. If you have a current escalation, or one that you need to escalate in the next few days, use that. Otherwise, think about a time when you have needed to escalate a topic to someone at work. If you did it by email, try to find that email so you can see exactly what you wrote.

If you have never escalated anything, or do not have anything you need to escalate now, make something up. Use a problem you wrote about in Section 1. Magnify the problem to the point it would need escalating. Then write out the escalation summary.

**NOTE**: Escalations happen when something has gone wrong. Either someone might get into trouble, a goal will be missed, something bad has, or will happen, and so on. Each of these comes with a bundle of emotions (guilt, worry, blame, frustration, etc.). By using the frameworks in The First Minute it is easier to keep the emotions out of the conversation. It is worth practicing this now, when things are calm. It will help you be better prepared when you get caught in the middle of a real escalation.

> ***Tip***: *If you are using the solution part of the structured summary to ask for help, the method is still valuable for escalations. It quickly defines the problem and allows more time to discuss possible solutions.*

*(Space for this activity is on the next page)*

## ESCALATION #1

**CONTEXT:** _____

**INTENT:** _____

**KEY MESSAGE:** _____

_____

**GOAL:** _____

_____

**PROBLEM:** _____

_____

**SOLUTION:** _____

_____

_____

_____

## ESCALATION #2

**CONTEXT:** _____

**INTENT:** _____

**KEY MESSAGE:** _____

_____

**GOAL:** _____

_____

**PROBLEM:** _____

_____

**SOLUTION:** _____

_____

_____

_____

## ESCALATION #3

**CONTEXT**: _____

**INTENT**: _____

**KEY MESSAGE**: _____
_____

**GOAL**: _____
_____

**PROBLEM**: _____
_____

**SOLUTION**: _____
_____
_____
_____

## QUESTIONS TO CONSIDER

- Do these methods reduce the number of opinions you share in an escalation?
- Is it easier to stick to factual statements and avoid describing opinions?
- Does the framework help keep emotions out of the topic?
- Does the focus on solutions, on what to do next, change your approach to escalations?

*(Blank page for notes)*

# END OF SECTION TWO

## Well done!

You have completed the activities for The First Minute.

In this section, you practiced applying The First Minute methods in the following situations:

- Emails
- Meeting invitations
- Status updates
- Escalations

You have seen how these methods can improve your communication by sing real examples from your own work. The activities gave you templates and scripts to use in your work communication. You can use these templates for the rest of your career.

The learning and practice doesn't stop here. If you keep applying the techniques to real conversations and emails it gets easier. Soon you will use The First Minute methods without thinking about it.

### NEXT STEPS:

1. Remember to visit www.chrisfenning.com/resources and download the extra templates and guides mentioned in this workbook.
2. Check out the bonus content below to get even more value from The First Minute.

*The remainder of this book contains additional blank templates for each activity in the workbook.*

---

**BONUS DOWNLOAD**

The First Minute methods are also powerful tools when it comes to interviews. Go to www.chrisfenning.com/tfminterviews and download a practical guide for applying these methods to give great interview answers.

*(Blank page for notes)*

# APPENDIX

**EXTRA PRACTICE TEMPLATES**

# FRAMING SINGLE TOPICS

**FRAMING**

**Context:** _____

**Intent:** _____

**Key message:** _____

_____

| Number of words used | |

**FRAMING**

**Context:** _____

**Intent:** _____

**Key message:** _____

_____

| Number of words used | |

**FRAMING**

**Context:** _____

**Intent:** _____

**Key message:** _____

_____

| Number of words used | |

**FRAMING**

**Context:** _____

**Intent:** _____

**Key message:** _____

_____

| Number of words used | |

**FRAMING**

**Context**: _____

**Intent**: _____

**Key message**: _____

_____

| Number of words used | |

**FRAMING**

**Context**: _____

**Intent**: _____

**Key message**: _____

_____

| Number of words used | |

**FRAMING**

**Context**: _____

**Intent**: _____

**Key message**: _____

_____

| Number of words used | |

**FRAMING**

**Context**: _____

**Intent**: _____

**Key message**: _____

_____

| Number of words used | |

# FRAMING MULTIPLE TOPICS

### FRAMING #1:

**Context**: _____

**Intent**: _____

**Key message**: _____

_____

### FRAMING #2:

**Context**: _____

**Intent**: _____

**Key message**: _____

_____

*Now write a summary framing that introduces the two topics as part of one conversation. More space is available to account for the extra information the summary framing will contain.*

### SUMMARY FRAMING

**Summary Context**: _____

_____

**Summary Intents**: _____

_____

_____

_____

**Key Messages**: _____

_____

_____

_____

_____

## FRAMING #1:

**Context**: _____

**Intent**: _____

**Key message**: _____

_____

## FRAMING #2:

**Context**: _____

**Intent**: _____

**Key message**: _____

_____

*Now write a summary framing that introduces the two topics as part of one conversation. More space is available to account for the extra information the summary framing will contain.*

## SUMMARY FRAMING

**Summary Context**: _____

_____

**Summary Intents**: _____

_____

_____

_____

**Key Messages**: _____

_____

_____

_____

_____

## FRAMING #1:

**Context:** _____

**Intent:** _____

**Key message:** _____

_____

## FRAMING #2:

**Context:** _____

**Intent:** _____

**Key message:** _____

_____

*Now write a summary framing that introduces the two topics as part of one conversation. More space is available to account for the extra information the summary framing will contain.*

## SUMMARY FRAMING

**Summary Context:** _____

_____

**Summary Intents:** _____

_____

_____

_____

**Key Messages:** _____

_____

_____

_____

## FRAMING #1:

**Context:** _____

**Intent:** _____

**Key message:** _____

_____

## FRAMING #2:

**Context:** _____

**Intent:** _____

**Key message:** _____

_____

*Now write a summary framing that introduces the two topics as part of one conversation. More space is available to account for the extra information the summary framing will contain.*

## SUMMARY FRAMING

**Summary Context:** _____

_____

**Summary Intents:** _____

_____

_____

_____

**Key Messages:** _____

_____

_____

_____

## FRAMING #1:

**Context:** _____

**Intent:** _____

**Key message:** _____

_____

## FRAMING #2:

**Context:** _____

**Intent:** _____

**Key message:** _____

_____

*Now write a summary framing that introduces the two topics as part of one conversation. More space is available to account for the extra information the summary framing will contain.*

## SUMMARY FRAMING

**Summary Context:** _____

_____

**Summary Intents:** _____

_____

_____

_____

**Key Messages:** _____

_____

_____

_____

_____

## FRAMING #1:

**Context:** _____

**Intent:** _____

**Key message:** _____

_____

## FRAMING #2:

**Context:** _____

**Intent:** _____

**Key message:** _____

_____

*Now write a summary framing that introduces the two topics as part of one conversation. More space is available to account for the extra information the summary framing will contain.*

## SUMMARY FRAMING

**Summary Context:** _____

_____

**Summary Intents:** _____

_____

_____

_____

**Key Messages:** _____

_____

_____

_____

_____

*(Blank page for notes)*

# STRUCTURED SUMMARY

## SUMMARY

**GOAL:** _____

_____

**PROBLEM:** _____

_____

**SOLUTION:** _____

_____

_____

_____

## SUMMARY

**GOAL:** _____

_____

**PROBLEM:** _____

_____

**SOLUTION:** _____

_____

_____

_____

*(More templates are available on the next page)*

## SUMMARY

**GOAL:** _____

_____

**PROBLEM:** _____

_____

**SOLUTION:** _____

_____

_____

_____

## SUMMARY

**GOAL:** _____

_____

**PROBLEM:** _____

_____

**SOLUTION:** _____

_____

_____

_____

## SUMMARY

**GOAL:** _____

_____

**PROBLEM:** _____

_____

**SOLUTION:** _____

_____

_____

_____

## SUMMARY

**GOAL**: _____

_____

**PROBLEM**: _____

_____

**SOLUTION**: _____

_____

_____

_____

## SUMMARY

**GOAL**: _____

_____

**PROBLEM**: _____

_____

**SOLUTION**: _____

_____

_____

_____

## SUMMARY

**GOAL**: _____

_____

**PROBLEM**: _____

_____

**SOLUTION**: _____

_____

_____

_____

*(Blank page for notes)*

# EMAILS

There are deliberately no email templates in this workbook appendix. This is because it is easy to practice structuring emails using your own email application. Start a blank email and send it to yourself.

An example email is shown below to help you see how the framing and structured summary are used to give a clear, easy to read message.

---

**To**: Diane@work.com

**Subject**: Website updates – priority decision needed

Hi Diane,

Can you help me with a priority order decision for the website development team?

**Goal**: The product team has asked us to fix a problem with the login screen on the website.

**Problem**: We have limited resources on our team, and another piece of work would have to move to a later delivery date for this change to occur.

**Solution**: Can you help me understand the priority for the following items? Which one can be delayed?

- Item #1: Layout changes for sidebar menus on the homepage
- Item #2: Automate the generation of the PDFs
- Item #3: Add a question form to the contact page

We have until Friday to decide on what to delay, so you have a couple of days. Please call me if you have any questions.

Thanks,

Chris

*(Blank page for notes)*

# MEETING INVITATIONS

## MEETING INVITATION

| To | |
|---|---|
| **Meeting date/time** | |
| **Subject** | |
| **Body of meeting invite** | |// spanning

| **Body of meeting invite** |
|---|
| **Meeting Purpose:** <br><br> **Meeting Output:** <br><br> **Summary info / Background / etc.:** <br><br><br><br> |

## MEETING INVITATION

| To | |
|---|---|
| **Meeting date/time** | |
| **Subject** | |

| **Body of meeting invite** |
|---|
| **Meeting Purpose:** <br><br> **Meeting Output:** <br><br> **Summary info / Background / etc.:** <br><br><br><br> |

## MEETING INVITATION

| To | |
|---|---|
| **Meeting date/time** | |
| **Subject** | |
| **Body of meeting invite** ||

**Meeting Purpose:**


**Meeting Output:**


**Summary info / Background / etc.:**




## MEETING INVITATION

| To | |
|---|---|
| **Meeting date/time** | |
| **Subject** | |
| **Body of meeting invite** ||

**Meeting Purpose:**


**Meeting Output:**


**Summary info / Background / etc.:**

## MEETING INVITATION

| To | |
|---|---|
| **Meeting date/time** | |
| **Subject** | |
| **Body of meeting invite** | |

**Meeting Purpose:**


**Meeting Output:**


**Summary info / Background / etc.:**




## MEETING INVITATION

| To | |
|---|---|
| **Meeting date/time** | |
| **Subject** | |
| **Body of meeting invite** | |

**Meeting Purpose:**


**Meeting Output:**


**Summary info / Background / etc.:**

*(Blank page for notes)*

# STATUS UPDATES

## STATUS UPDATE

**CONTEXT:** _____

**INTENT:** _____

**KEY MESSAGE:** _____

_____

**GOAL:** _____

_____

**PROBLEM:** _____

_____

**SOLUTION:** _____

_____

_____

_____

**VALIDATION CHECKPOINT QUESTION:** _____

_____

## STATUS UPDATE

**CONTEXT:** _____

**INTENT:** _____

**KEY MESSAGE:** _____

_____

**GOAL:** _____

_____

**PROBLEM:** _____

_____

**SOLUTION:** _____

_____

_____

_____

**VALIDATION CHECKPOINT QUESTION:** _____

_____

## STATUS UPDATE

**CONTEXT:** _____

**INTENT:** _____

**KEY MESSAGE:** _____

_____

**GOAL:** _____

_____

**PROBLEM:** _____

_____

**SOLUTION:** _____

_____

_____

_____

**VALIDATION CHECKPOINT QUESTION:** _____

_____

## STATUS UPDATE

**CONTEXT:** _____

**INTENT:** _____

**KEY MESSAGE:** _____

_____

**GOAL:** _____

_____

**PROBLEM:** _____

_____

**SOLUTION:** _____

_____

_____

_____

**VALIDATION CHECKPOINT QUESTION:** _____

_____

# ESCALATIONS

## ESCALATION

**CONTEXT:** _____

**INTENT:** _____

**KEY MESSAGE:** _____
_____

**GOAL:** _____
_____

**PROBLEM:** _____
_____

**SOLUTION:** _____
_____
_____
_____

## ESCALATION

**CONTEXT:** _____

**INTENT:** _____

**KEY MESSAGE:** _____
_____

**GOAL:** _____
_____

**PROBLEM:** _____
_____

**SOLUTION:** _____
_____
_____
_____

## ESCALATION

**CONTEXT:** _____

**INTENT:** _____

**KEY MESSAGE:** _____
_____

**GOAL:** _____
_____

**PROBLEM:** _____
_____

**SOLUTION:** _____
_____
_____
_____

## ESCALATION

**CONTEXT:** _____

**INTENT:** _____

**KEY MESSAGE:** _____
_____

**GOAL:** _____
_____

**PROBLEM:** _____
_____

**SOLUTION:** _____
_____
_____
_____

## ESCALATION

**CONTEXT:** _____

**INTENT:** _____

**KEY MESSAGE:** _____

_____

**GOAL:** _____

_____

**PROBLEM:** _____

_____

**SOLUTION:** _____

_____

_____

_____

## ESCALATION

**CONTEXT:** _____

**INTENT:** _____

**KEY MESSAGE:** _____

_____

**GOAL:** _____

_____

**PROBLEM:** _____

_____

**SOLUTION:** _____

_____

_____

_____

***Did you enjoy this book?***

The best way to thank an author is to post a review on Amazon!

(Please and thank you!)

www.ingramcontent.com/pod-product-compliance
Lightning Source LLC
Chambersburg PA
CBHW051247110526
44588CB00025B/2907